D1755686

# The Amazing Panini Cookbook

The Absolute Best Sandwich Recipes to Enjoy

By

Angel Burns

© 2022 Angel Burns, All Rights Reserved.

# License Notices

This book or parts thereof might not be reproduced in any format for personal or commercial use without the written permission of the author. Possession and distribution of this book by any means without said permission is prohibited by law.

All content is for entertainment purposes and the author accepts no responsibility for any damages, commercially or personally, caused by following the content.

# Table of Contents

Introduction .................................................................................................... 6

Panini Recipes ................................................................................................ 9

    1. Marshmallow Panini .............................................................................. 10

    2. Choco Rich Panini ................................................................................ 12

    3. Cheesy Prosciutto Panini ...................................................................... 14

    4. Smoked Gouda Turkey Panini ............................................................... 16

    5. Buttered Scallion Soup with Cheddar Panini ........................................... 18

    6. Peanut Butter Panini ............................................................................. 21

    7. Chocolate Banana Panini ...................................................................... 23

    8. Apple Turkey Panini .............................................................................. 25

    9. Double Chocolate Panini ....................................................................... 27

    10. Panini Loaded with Turkey .................................................................. 29

    11. Tandoori Chicken Panini ..................................................................... 31

    12. Provolone Turkey Panini ..................................................................... 34

    13. Simple California Style Panini ............................................................. 36

    14. Topped Banana Panini ........................................................................ 38

    15. Lamb Panini Burger ............................................................................ 40

    16. Muffuletta Panini ................................................................................ 42

    17. Bánh Mì Panini ................................................................................... 44

    18. Southwestern Turkey Panini ................................................................ 46

    19. The Ultimate Thanksgiving Reuben Panini ........................................... 48

    20. Vegan Pepper Jack Roasted Pepper Panini ........................................... 50

    21. Peach Caprese Panini .......................................................................... 52

22. Mixed Berry French Toast Panini ............................................................. 54

23. Prosciutto and Egg Bagel Panini ............................................................. 57

24. A Perfect Italian Panini ............................................................................ 59

25. Ham and Pear Panini ............................................................................... 61

26. Simple Prosciutto and Roasted Pepper Panini ......................................... 63

27. Peach Caprese Panini .............................................................................. 65

28. Tuna and Bacon Melting Panini .............................................................. 67

29. Monterey Artichoke Panini ..................................................................... 69

30. Garden Chicken Panini ........................................................................... 71

31. Curried Chicken Panini ........................................................................... 73

32. Turkey, Bacon and Feta Panini ............................................................... 75

33. Corned Beef Cheddar Panini ................................................................... 77

34. Margherita Panini .................................................................................... 79

35. Maple Blackberry Panini ......................................................................... 81

36. Bacon, Asparagus, and Mayo Panini ...................................................... 83

37. Zesty Crabmeat Panini ............................................................................ 85

38. Roasted Vegetable Panini Bite ................................................................ 87

39. Eggplant Panini ....................................................................................... 89

40. Sourdough Chipotle Chicken Panini ....................................................... 91

41. Panzanella Panini .................................................................................... 93

42. Italian-Style Tuna Melt ........................................................................... 95

43. Cheddar – Turkey Panini ........................................................................ 97

44. Turkey & Swiss Reuben Sandwich ......................................................... 99

45. Deli lamb Mayo Panini ........................................................................... 101

46. Caramelized Onion Panini ...................................................................... 103

47. Sausage Spinach Panini .................................................................. 105

48. Spelt Spinach Mushroom Panini ..................................................... 107

49. Fig and Artichoke Panini ................................................................ 109

50. Chocolate Panini ............................................................................ 111

51. Southwestern Panini ...................................................................... 113

52. Chicken Florentine Panini .............................................................. 115

53. Apple Pie Panini a La Mode ........................................................... 117

54. Banana Brûlée Croissant Panini .................................................... 119

55. Mallow, Hazelnut, and Banana ...................................................... 121

56. PB&J Panini ................................................................................... 123

57. Grilled Chicken Panini .................................................................... 125

58. Kicking Bacon Panini ..................................................................... 127

59. Cordon Bleu Panini ........................................................................ 129

Conclusion ................................................................................................ 131

About the Author ...................................................................................... 132

Author's Afterthoughts ............................................................................. 133

# Introduction

***What is a Panini?***

A Panini is a sandwich made from sliced bread, filled with your choice of meat, cheese, vegetables, or other ingredients, and grilled on both sides. You can make a Panini on your own but buy bakery-style bread that can be sliced into long thin slices to make it easy. You will also need to use short stacks of buttered bread slices to hold each sandwich in one hand. If you use regular sliced bread, you'll need to butter the slices, cut them in half and stack the two halves on the grill. This can make a Panini difficult to hold. If you are making a Panini for one person, it is best not to make it too big. Each sandwich should be served on its plate and cut in half before serving. You do not want a lot of bread if you are eating alone because that can get very heavy and hard to eat in one bite.

When you buy Panini-style sandwich bread, look for one of good quality. This can be hard to determine when you purchase some cheap brands. While you can use any type of bread to make Paninis, it is best to use bakery-style bread because it is made better and does not get as soggy if it is not heated properly.

*Choosing a great Panini recipe*

When you choose a recipe for your Panini, consider the ingredients used to make it. If you don't like too many spicy foods, then stay away from recipes with hot pepper or other hot sauces. You will also want to stay away from some fish recipes because they can get messy even when cooked on a grill. When you choose your recipe, think about how easy it will be to handle. The ingredients should also be easy to find, and you shouldn't have to worry about what you are using.

*What benefits do you enjoy?*

Enjoying a Panini is quite an experience. You will enjoy the crunchy texture of the bread, and you will be able to pick up your sandwich and eat it like a regular hot dog or sandwich. It is easy to cut your sandwich in half or thirds if you want to see what's inside. Once you make your first Panini, you will find it quite tasty. You can even choose different fillings and even use different kinds of bread when you make them yourself. You will change the recipe a little each time you make it for variety.

*Be creative*

Once you have tried a few easy Panini recipes, you will find that you can start using your creativity to come up with new ideas. For instance, if you enjoy spicy foods, it is easy to add some salsa or blended peppers and chilis to your bread. You can take some of your favorite ingredients, roll them into a tortilla or Pita pocket, and grill them until hot on both sides. You can also use the meal ideas for other meals and use them in your Panini recipes.

*Tips for making great Panini recipes*

When you make a Panini, be sure to use good ingredients. Use hearty meats such as steak or chicken to make a sandwich that will hold up well. When shaping your sandwich, do not just slather on the cheese because it will melt into the bread and turn soggy if it is moist. You'll find that if you use good cheese, the bread will hold up well and keep its crustiness. Use good meat for your Panini.

If you have never made a sandwich, you have no idea how to handle the ingredients. Always be sure to cover the sandwich and then press down firmly on top of it so that it does not come apart when you slice it in half or cut some of it into small pieces.

Once you finish your Panini on one side, you should be careful when you flip it because it is easy to get oil and other ingredients all over the place. Remember, the grill is hot, and you don't want that hot liquid to come splashing out. Instead, use a spatula to get underneath your sandwich and then turn it over carefully.

Some people like to heat sliced tomatoes or other vegetables on the grill and put them in the middle of the meat, so it helps keep everything warm. Paninis are great for entertaining because you can put all of the ingredients together and then put them on the grill, and your guests can come to the table whenever they are done.

A Panini recipe is a great way to enjoy your lunch or dinner. They taste better than other sandwiches because they have nice crusty bread. Look through these recipes and find one that is perfect for you. If you already enjoy eating Paninis and know how to make them, then you can use these recipes for inspiration to create your own.

# Panini Recipes

These are delicious recipes for your Panini grill. You get to enjoy a unique experience and enjoy great flavors.

# 1. Marshmallow Panini

These soft Panini will leave you wanting more and more. They take a short duration to cook and prepare.

**Servings:** 2

**Preparation Time:** 10 Minutes

**Ingredients:**

- Hershey's chocolate spread
- 2 slices white bread
- 1 toasted jumbo marshmallow

**Instructions:**

Preheat your Panini grill, then spray it with oil.

Spread the Hershey's on the bread.

Add the marshmallow, then put another slice of bread on it to cover.

Cook the sandwich on the grill for about two minutes on every side.

## 2. Choco Rich Panini

Who does not love chocolates? The recipe coated with chocolate will soothe your taste buds as they are very delicious.

**Servings:** 2

**Preparation Time:** 10 Minutes

**Ingredients:**

- 2 oz. chopped semisweet Chocolate
- 4 white bread slices

**Instructions:**

Place the chocolate pieces between two slices of bread.

Cook in a panini press while closed for about two minutes on every side.

When the chocolate melts, remove it from the Panini.

# 3. Cheesy Prosciutto Panini

These nutritious ingredients add up to form a fantastic sandwich that you can serve on those lazy weekend mornings.

**Servings:** 1

**Preparation Time:** 10 Minutes

**Ingredients:**

- 3 oz. thinly sliced brussels sprouts
- 2 thinly sliced prosciutto
- 2 slices of fresh bread
- 2 tbsp caramelized onions
- Olive oil
- Salt
- 1 ½ oz. thinly sliced fresh mozzarella

**Instructions:**

In a pan, heat the olive oil.

Add in the sprouts as you stir them gently.

Sprinkle the sprouts with salt, then cook it on high heat for a minute.

Preheat your panini grill, then grease it.

Take a slice of the bread. Add the onions, mozzarella, sprouts, prosciutto, then top with another piece.

Slightly oil both sides of the slices.

Transfer the sandwich into the panini grill, then cook for about six minutes until all the cheese melts.

Serve the sandwich in a diagonal shape.

# 4. Smoked Gouda Turkey Panini

The combination of turkey and other ingredients makes this recipe superb. It is suitable for the whole family as it is crunchy and sweet.

**Servings:** 1

**Preparation Time:** 20 Minutes

**Ingredients:**

- 1 slice smoked gouda cheese
- 2 slice artisan bread
- 2 tbsp cranberry sauce
- 4 slices butterball white turkey meat
- 4 slices cored, peeled, and sliced apples

**Instructions:**

On a bread slice, place the turkey.

Add the cheese and sauce to the turkey, followed by apple slices, then cover with the other slice.

Preheat your panini press.

Transfer the sandwich to the Panini.

Cook for 10 minutes.

Serve warm.

# 5. Buttered Scallion Soup with Cheddar Panini

It is a satisfying panini recipe that one can take as lunch or dinner. The soup is sweet and nutritious for the whole family.

**Servings:** 4

**Preparation Time:** 30 Minutes

**Ingredients:**

- 3 tbsp butter
- 3 boxes (10 oz. each) frozen peas
- 1 ½ cups shredded sharp white cheddar
- Coarse salt and ground pepper
- 4 thinly sliced scallions with white and green parts separated
- 1 can (14.5 oz.) reduced-sodium chicken broth
- 8 slices rye sandwich bread
- 1 tbsp fresh lemon juice

**Instructions:**

In a saucepan, melt the butter.

Add the scallion whites and cook them until they become soft.

Add the broth, peas, and 3 cups of water.

Boil the mixture at simmering heat, allowing them to cook until they become tender.

Remove from the heat, then set them aside.

In a separate bowl, mix the scallion greens and cheddar.

Brush a slice of bread with the oil, then place the cheddar mix between them.

Top the cheddar mix with the other slice of bread.

Preheat your grill, then cook the sandwich in it.

Cook until the sandwich becomes golden in color and crisp.

In a blender, process the pea mixture until it becomes smooth. Add lemon juice and seasonings.

Slice the sandwich into finger strips.

Serve it with the soup.

# 6. Peanut Butter Panini

It is an easy and simple recipe to cook. The recipe can serve as a perfect dessert for the family. The addition of peanuts and marshmallows makes the recipe delicious and outrageously sweet.

**Servings:** 4

**Prep Time:** 15 minutes

**Ingredients:**

- 4 halved split bagel thins
- ¼ cup milk chocolate chunks
- ½ cup mini marshmallows
- ¼ cup creamy peanut butter
- 4 tbsp unsalted butter

**Instructions:**

Preheat a grill pan over medium heat.

On a half bagel, spread peanut butter.

Top it with the chocolate chunks alongside marshmallows.

Top the bagel with a second half to cover the ingredients.

Melt butter on the grill, then cook the bagels until the chocolate and marshmallows begin to melt.

Allow it to cool.

Serve and enjoy.

# 7. Chocolate Banana Panini

The chocolate banana panini is a recipe that you can take a short time to prepare. The taste is irresistible, and even for the picky eaters, they will love it. It can serve as a dessert any time of the day.

**Servings:** 1

**Prep Time:** 10 minutes

**Ingredients:**

- 1 oz. white chocolate chips
- 1/4 tsp peanut butter
- 2 bread slices
- 1 sliced banana

**Instructions:**

Preheat your panini press.

On a slice of bread, spread the peanut butter.

Top it with chocolate chips.

Top it with the banana slices on the other slice, then place it over the other slice.

Grill it in the panini maker for 4 minutes.

# 8. Apple Turkey Panini

No one can resist this perfect panini combination of green apples and cheddar cheese. It is a great recipe for both kids and adults. Following this recipe will help you avoid the use of frozen items. The result is a nutritious, healthy, and delicious Panini.

**Servings:** 2

**Prep Time:** 10 minutes

**Ingredients:**

- 4 slices whole-grain bread
- 8 thinly sliced roasted turkey
- 2 tbsp Dijon mustard
- 1 thinly sliced green apple
- 4 tbsp butter with canola oil
- 8 slices sharp cheddar cheese

**Instructions:**

Preheat your grill.

Use butter along with canola oil, lightly oil the outer sides of the bread slices.

Spread the mustard, then top with the apple slices on one slice.

Top the ingredients with the turkey slices.

Place the cheese over the turkey, then cover with the other slice of bread.

Cook the sandwich on the grill for 5 minutes.

Remove it from the grill, then cut it into two.

# 9. Double Chocolate Panini

For chocolate lovers, this is the ideal Panini for you. The recipe takes a short time to prepare and is filled with both creaminess and crunchiness.

**Servings:** 4

**Prep Time:** 12 minutes

**Ingredients:**

- 8 slices bread
- 8 tbsp Nutella
- 4 tbsp mini chocolate chips

**Instructions:**

Preheat your panini press.

Spread the Nutella over two slices of bread.

Spread the chocolate chips on one slice, then cover it with the other slice.

Repeat with the remaining slices, then place the sandwiches over the grill.

Close the lid, then cook for about 2 minutes.

# 10. Panini Loaded with Turkey

The perfect and ideal thanksgiving panini recipe is this one with turkey. You can also try this recipe for other occasions like parties or get-togethers.

**Servings:** 1

**Prep Time:** 10 minutes

**Ingredients:**

- 2 slices bread
- 1 oz. goat cheese
- 5 sage leaves
- 4 few slices of turkey
- 1 tbsp butter
- 3 tbsp cranberry sauce
- 1 slice Muenster cheese

**Instructions:**

Preheat your Panini.

Spread the butter on the outer parts of the slices of bread.

One after the other, take a slice of bread and cover it with all the ingredients.

Top it with the other slice.

Cook the sandwich in the Panini for 5 minutes.

# 11. Tandoori Chicken Panini

In India, Tandoori chicken is one of the best dishes. The recipe is about trying something new with a mix of Panini and chicken. It takes time to prepare this meal, but the outcome is satisfying. The blend of Indian spices will give you a feel of a short tour of India.

**Servings:** 6

**Prep Time:** 3 Hours 25 minutes

**Ingredients:**

- 1 and 1/3 lb. boneless and skinless chicken breasts
- ¼ cup reduced-sodium chicken broth
- 6 chopped green onions
- 2 tsp minced fresh ginger root
- 2 garlic cloves, minced
- ¼ tsp cayenne pepper
- ¼ tsp ground turmeric
- ¼ tsp salt
- 1 tsp paprika
- 6 tbsp chutney
- 6 naan flatbreads

**Instructions:**

Add the chicken, garlic cloves, chicken broth, ginger root, salt, paprika, turmeric, and cayenne pepper in a slow cooker.

Cover the cooker, then cook for 3 hours until the ingredients become tender.

Shred the chicken, then add the onions.

Stir well to mix.

On one side of every naan, pour chutney.

Top it with the chicken mixture.

Cover the first naan with the remaining one.

Transfer the sandwiches to the panini maker.

Cook for 8 minutes until it becomes golden brown.

Divide the sandwich in half.

Serve and enjoy.

# 12. Provolone Turkey Panini

The delicacy will brighten your morning as it is crunchy, delicious, and full of flavor. Try this recipe for the family breakfast and watch their faces fill up with happiness.

**Servings:** 1

**Preparation Time:** 5 minutes

**Ingredients:**

- 2 slices bread
- 3 slices turkey
- 1 jarred roasted red pepper
- 2 slices provolone cheese
- Olive oil

**Instructions:**

On a bread slice, place the turkey, then top it with the cheese and pepper.

Cover it with the other bread slice.

Preheat a panini grill. Grease it with olive oil.

Transfer the sandwich onto the grill.

Cook it until both sides of the sandwich turn golden brown.

# 13. Simple California Style Panini

It is a simple recipe to prepare. It is filling and an excellent snack for those busy days.

**Servings:** 4

**Preparation Time:** 30 Minutes

**Ingredients:**

- 2 halved and sliced avocados
- 1/3 cup smoked, julienned, and sun-dried tomato
- 2 tbsp diced red onions
- 2 cups lightly packed baby spinach
- 16 oz. halved ciabatta rolls

**Instructions:**

Preheat your panini press.

On the bottom half of every ciabatta, place the avocado slices. Top with the onion, tomatoes, and spinach.

Transfer the sandwiches into the panini press.

Cook for 4 minutes.

Serve and enjoy.

# 14. Topped Banana Panini

Any time you add a banana to your recipe, you can never go wrong. The cuisine is suitable for both children and adults.

**Servings:** 6

**Preparation Time:** 20 Minutes

**Ingredients:**

- 3 sliced ripe bananas
- 12 slices whole-wheat bread
- 1 cup chocolate hazelnut spread
- 16 tbsp softened unsalted butter
- 3 tbsp confectioners' sugar

**Instructions:**

Preheat your grill, then grease the grate lightly.

In a bowl, mash the bananas, ensuring they become smooth.

Place six slices of bread on a platter, then divide the banana mash on each one. Top with hazelnut spread.

Cover the slices with banana with the remaining bread slices.

Spread the butter on both sandwich sides.

Cook the sandwiches on the grill until both sides turn golden brown.

Remove from the grill, then dust the sandwiches with the sugar.

Serve when hot.

# 15. Lamb Panini Burger

The spices in this recipe compliment the lamb, thus resulting in great favor. The lamb releases fat and juices as the panini cooks, making the bread crispy and nice.

**Servings:** 8

**Preparation Time:** 20 Minutes

**Ingredients:**

- 2 ½ lbs. shoulder lamb, ground
- 1 finely chopped medium onion
- ¾ cup chopped fresh flat-leaf parsley
- 1 tbsp coriander, ground
- ¾ tsp cumin, ground
- ½ tsp cinnamon, ground
- 2 tsp kosher salt
- 1 ½ tsp black pepper, ground
- ¼ cup olive oil, plus extra for grilling
- 8 thick medium pita bread with pockets

**Instructions:**

Mix the parsley, coriander, cumin, cinnamon, black pepper, oil, salt, onion and lamb using a fork.

Let the meat rest while covered for about one hour.

Fill the pitas with the meat mixture.

Cook the sandwiches on medium heat for about 10 minutes as you flip them halfway.

Ensure the lamb gets to cook through, and the bread becomes crunchy.

# 16. Muffuletta Panini

It is a unique panini recipe tracing its classical roots from New Orleans, the food capital. The salad topping and pork cuts mix to bring out flavors in this delicacy.

**Servings:** 4

**Preparation Time:** 15 Minutes

**Ingredients:**

- Softened butter
- 8 slices rustic bread
- 16 thin slices provolone cheese
- ½ cup drained olive salad
- 6 oz. thinly sliced black forest ham
- 6 oz. sliced mortadella
- 4 oz. sliced Genoa salami

**Instructions:**

On both sides of the rustic slices, spread the butter.

On 4 slices, place 2 cheese pieces.

Top with olive salad, salami, ham, and mortadella.

Top the ingredients with the remaining cheese pieces.

Cover with ingredients with the remaining bread slices.

Cook the sandwiches on moderate heat for about 4 minutes as you flip them halfway.

Ensure the bread turns brown, and all the cheese gets to melt.

# 17. Bánh Mì Panini

It is a unique sandwich from Vietnam that has a combination of some French and Vietnamese flavors. It takes a short duration to prepare, making it an easy dessert or snack.

**Servings:** 1

**Prep Time:** 14 Minutes

**Ingredients:**

- 1 petite baguette roll
- 1 cup mayonnaise
- 1/2 tbsp Maggi Seasoning sauce
- 1 lb. sliced boldly flavored cooked, pork liver pâté, all at room temperature
- 4 thin seeded cucumber strips
- 3 coarsely chopped sprigs of cilantro
- 4 thin slices of jalapeno chili
- ¼ cup daikon and carrot pickle

**Instructions:**

Divide the bread into half, then remove some of the soft parts of both pieces.

Spread in the mayonnaise into both bread pieces.

Coat it with the Maggi seasoning sauce lightly.

Top with the meat, then cucumbers, jalapenos, cilantro, and finally pickles.

Cook the sandwiches for 5 minutes as you flip them halfway over medium heat.

# 18. Southwestern Turkey Panini

If you are looking for a sandwich recipe with all kinds of southwestern flavor, this is the recipe for you. It has a depth in flavor thanks to the Colby jack cheese. In addition, the avocado and chipotle mayo give it creaminess and a kick, respectively.

**Servings:** 2

**Preparation Time:** 20 Minutes

**Ingredients:**

- 1 peeled and seeded medium avocado
- ½ tbsp finely chopped cilantro leaves
- ½ tsp lime juice
- 4 slices large sourdough bread
- 1 tbsp chipotle mayonnaise
- 4 slices tomato
- 8 slices Colby Jack cheese
- 8 slices blackened oven-roasted turkey breast
- Salt and pepper

**Instructions:**

In a bowl, mix the lime juice, avocado, and cilantro. Mash the mixture, then add pepper and salt to taste.

On every bread piece, spread the mayonnaise on each side.

With the mayonnaise side of two bread pieces facing up, place cheese, turkey, tomato, avocado mixture, turkey, and cheese in that order.

Cover the ingredients with the remaining bread pieces with the mayonnaise side contacting the cheese.

Cook the sandwiches on medium heat for 6 minutes.

Flip the sandwich halfway to ensure that the bread is well toasted, and the cheese gets to melt.

# 19. The Ultimate Thanksgiving Reuben Panini

Are you having thanksgiving leftovers? Put them to use as you prepare this delicacy. The cranberries make a perfect fit as it acts as a substitution for turkey for corned beef.

**Servings:** 4

**Preparation Time:** 25 Minutes

**Ingredients:**

- 1/3 cup mayonnaise
- 2 tbsp cranberry sauce
- 2 tsp freshly grated horseradish
- 1 tsp Worcestershire sauce
- Kosher salt and black pepper
- 2 cups shredded green cabbage
- 8 slices rye bread
- 8 slices Swiss cheese
- ¾ lb. thinly sliced carved turkey
- 2 tbsp melted butter

**Instructions:**

Using a whisk, mix the mayonnaise, cranberry, horseradish, and Worcestershire sauce in a bowl.

Add salt and pepper, then add the cabbage. Mix well to ensure the cabbage gets to coat.

Place the cheese, turkey, slaw, turkey layer, and cheese once again on a bread slice.

Cover the ingredients with the remaining slices of bread.

Apply butter to the top and bottom of the sandwich.

On medium heat, cook the sandwich for 7 minutes as you flip them halfway.

Ensure the bread is well toasted and the cheese gets to melt.

Serve and enjoy.

# 20. Vegan Pepper Jack Roasted Pepper Panini

As the name suggests, this recipe suits all vegans. It is spicy, making it have great flavor. The addition of cheese brings in the Panini's creaminess while the Harissa adds heat to the meal.

**Servings:** 1

**Preparation Time:** 15 Minutes

**Ingredients:**

- 2 slices bread
- 2 tsp vegan buttery spread
- 5 thin tomato slices
- ¼ cup fresh basil leaves
- ¼ cup vegan pepper jack cheese shreds
- 3 thin slices roasted red peppers
- ½ cup baby spinach
- 1 tsp black pepper
- 1 tsp Harissa

**Instructions:**

Using the buttery, spread it on the outside of each slice of bread.

Spread Harissa on the opposite side, which will serve as an inner part of the sandwich.

On a slice, arrange the ingredients starting with tomatoes, spinach, basil, peppers, black pepper, then vegan cheese.

Cover the ingredients with the other slice, with the harissa side touching the cheese.

In the panini press, cook the sandwich on moderate heat for 4 minutes as you flip it halfway.

Remove the sandwich once the bread is brown and all the cheese gets to melt.

# 21. Peach Caprese Panini

Ever had a Caprese salad? Thanks to the peach, this recipe has a similar taste but a sweet twist: mozzarella cream, basil, and vinegar balance off the taste.

**Servings:** 1

**Preparation Time:** 15 Minutes

**Ingredients:**

- 1 split French deli roll
- 1 ½ tsp balsamic vinegar
- 2 slices mozzarella cheese
- 1 sliced small heirloom tomato
- 4 fresh basil leaves
- Olive oil
- 1 small sliced peach

**Instructions:**

On the inner side of the bread pieces, sprinkle the vinegar.

Brush the outside of the bread pieces using olive oil.

Arrange the ingredients on the bottom bread piece, starting with mozzarella pieces, peach slices, tomato slices, basil leaves, and finally, the other cheese piece.

Cover the ingredients with the remaining bread piece.

Cook the sandwich in the Panini for 5 minutes on medium heat as you flip it halfway.

Serve and enjoy.

# 22. Mixed Berry French Toast Panini

It is a recipe with all the berry flavors that one can want. The blackberry and raspberry flavors get enhanced by the creaminess of the cheese.

**Servings:** 4

**Prep Time:** 25 Minutes

**Ingredients:**

- 6 large eggs
- 1 cup whole milk
- ½ cup heavy cream cheese
- ¼ cup fresh orange juice
- 2 tbsp vanilla extract
- 2 tbsp cognac
- 2 tbsp granulated sugar
- ½ tsp ground cinnamon
- 1 pinch freshly grated nutmeg
- 1 tsp salt
- 8 slices Texas toast
- 1 cup blackberries
- 1 cup raspberries
- 1 tbsp confectioners' sugar
- ¼ cup pure maple syrup

**Instructions:**

On the inside of the bread pieces, spread the cream cheese.

Place the berries on 4 of the slices, then cover with the remaining pieces of bread.

Whisk the eggs, vanilla, cinnamon, milk, salt, cognac, nutmeg, orange juice, and sugar in a bowl.

Place the sandwich in a shallow baking dish, then cover it with the egg mixture.

Let it rest for 10 minutes.

Preheat your sandwich maker.

Cook the Panini for 7 minutes as you flip it halfway through.

Remove from the sandwich maker, then top with the maple syrup and confectioners' sugar.

# 23. Prosciutto and Egg Bagel Panini

The recipe is suitable for breakfast for both adults and kids. The prosciutto adds saltiness to the cheese. The eggs also add a rich flavor to the Panini, making it a delicious dish.

**Servings:** 2

**Prep Time:** 15 Minutes

**Ingredients:**

- 2 eggs
- 2 everything bagels
- 2 tbsp mayonnaise
- 2 slices American cheese
- 4 slices prosciutto
- 2 handfuls of baby arugula
- Kosher salt
- Ground black pepper
- Olive oil
- 2 tsp butter

**Instructions:**

Using a whisk, beat the egg, then add pepper and salt.

In a skillet, melt the butter. Push the eggs across the pan using a spoon.

Cook the eggs for 2 minutes until they become set.

Divide the bagels into half, then spread mayonnaise in the bagels.

Add the eggs, cheese, arugula, and prosciutto to the bagel.

Cover the ingredients with the rest of the bagel.

Brush both the bottom and top of the bagel with the oil.

Cook the sandwich for 4 minutes as you flip it halfway.

# 24. A Perfect Italian Panini

If you fancy Italian ingredients, this recipe is a to-go recipe. The preparation and cook time is short, making it the best choice for dinner or breakfast.

**Servings:** 6

**Preparation Time:** 12 minutes

**Ingredients:**

- ¼ cup finely chopped stuffed green olives
- ½ cup finely chopped marinated pickled vegetables
- 1 ½ cup cream cheese with mozzarella
- 2 ½ oz. sliced salami
- 6 halved Italian buns
- 4 ¼ oz. sliced deli ham
- 1 tbsp olive oil

**Instructions:**

Mix the vegetables and olives, then set them aside.

On the bottom half of every bun, spread the cheese.

Layer meat, vegetable mix, and then top with the remaining cheese on the cheese.

Cover the ingredients with the other bun half.

Brush the buns with olive oil.

Grill in your Panini for about 5 minutes.

## 25. Ham and Pear Panini

Adding pear to your ingredients will add more sweetness to the Panini. It also enriches the flavor making it more fulfilling.

**Servings:** 2

**Preparation Time:** 10 minutes

**Ingredients:**

- 4 bread slices
- 1 tbsp mustard
- 6 ham slices
- 1 peeled and thinly sliced pear
- 1 cup mozzarella cheese, shredded
- 2 dashes of black pepper
- 1 tbsp of margarine

**Instructions:**

On the two bottom slices. Spread the mustard.

On every slice, put half of the slices of ham, then pear, then pepper, and finally cheese.

Cover the ingredients with the remaining bread slices. Then, spread margarine on the outer sides of the sandwich.

Grill your sandwich in a panini presser for 5 minutes until the bread turns brown

Serve and enjoy.

# 26. Simple Prosciutto and Roasted Pepper Panini

You prepare a recipe when you are clueless about what to cook for breakfast or dinner.

**Servings:** 2

**Preparation Time:** 10 minutes

**Ingredients:**

- 2 oz. sliced prosciutto
- 6 slices roasted red pepper
- 2 slices fresh mozzarella
- 2 tbsp basil pesto
- 4 slices French bread
- Olive oil

**Instructions:**

Brush the oil on the bottom side of the bread slices, then place the bottoms on your grill with the oiled part down.

Spread the pesto on the bottom, then prosciutto, pepper, then cheese.

Cover with the other slices as you press them down.

Grill the sandwich for 4 minutes.

# 27. Peach Caprese Panini

Nothing makes the kitchen lively being adventurous with your recipes. So, prepare this recipe to get new flavors that will bring tingling sensation to your family's taste buds.

**Servings:** 2 servings

**Preparation Time:** 10 minutes

**Ingredients:**

- ½ loaf Italian bread
- 2 slices prosciutto
- 1 deseeded and sliced peach
- 4 oz. sliced mozzarella
- 6 fresh basil leaves
- Olive oil

**Instructions:**

Divide the bread into half horizontally, then cut it into two slices.

Place the prosciutto, peach, basil, and cheese on the bottom slices.

Cover with the remaining slices.

Oil the outer sides of the slices.

Grill in the Panini for 5 minutes.

# 28. Tuna and Bacon Melting Panini

There is no excuse for not trying Panini as Tuna goes perfectly with any sandwich type.

**Servings:** 2

**Preparation Time:** 10 minutes

**Ingredients:**

- 16 oz. drained canned tuna
- ½ minced rib of celery
- 3 tbsp mayonnaise
- Salt and pepper
- 4 slices sandwich bread
- 4 slices cooked bacon
- 1 sliced tomato
- 4 slices mozzarella cheese

**Instructions:**

Mix the tuna, celery, mayonnaise, pepper, and salt in a bowl.

Apply some mayonnaise on two bread slices, add a layer of bacon, salad, tomato, and finally two cheese slices on each bread slice.

Cover the two filled bread slices with the remaining slices.

Grill the sandwich for about 5 minutes.

# 29. Monterey Artichoke Panini

If you are looking for a nutrient and fresh sandwich recipe, this is the ideal one. The combination of cheesy slices and veggies makes this recipe complete. In addition, the recipe takes a short time to prepare and is suitable for the whole family.

**Servings:** 2

**Preparation Time:** 25 minutes

**Ingredients:**

- 4 slices multigrain bread
- 4 thick slices of Monterey low-fat jack cheese
- ½ cup rinsed, drained, halved, and heart-shaped artichoke water-packed
- ½ cup freshly picked baby spinach
- 4 slices fresh and finely sliced tomato
- 1 tbsps. softened butter

**Instructions:**

Top two bread pieces with the cheese.

Layer both sides with ¼ cup of the artichokes, then ¼ cup spinach, 2 slices of tomato, then cover with the rest of the cheese.

Cover with the remaining slices of bread, then on their outer parts, apply butter.

Transfer to a panini maker, then cook for 4 minutes until the bread turns golden brown.

Serve and enjoy.

# 30. Garden Chicken Panini

The recipe gets its decent taste from the combination of giardiniera pickles and chicken. If you know of the giardiniera pickle, then you will understand it is Italian. It adds to the sandwich's sour taste making it unique from other panini recipes.

**Serving:** 4

**Preparation Time:** 20 minutes

**Ingredients:**

- 2 packs (12 oz. each) refrigerated breaded chicken breast
- ¼ cup softened unsalted butter
- 8 slices freshly baked Italian bread
- ¼ cup tomato puree
- ¼ cup giardiniera
- 8 slices part-skim mozzarella cheese

**Instructions:**

Prepare the chicken tenders according to the instructions on its package.

Take the slices of bread, then butter aside on each.

Transfer 4 of the slices to a panini grill.

Add a tablespoon of the puree, three chicken pieces, giardiniera, and cheese to the slices.

Cover the ingredients with the remaining slices of bread.

Cook the sandwich on both sides until the bread turns golden brown.

# 31. Curried Chicken Panini

It is a very dripping and saucy panini recipe. However, chopping the chicken makes it a better filling ingredient, and you can go further by introducing mayonnaise as a topping to make it more delicious.

**Serving:** 4

**Preparation time:** 20 minutes

**Ingredients:**

- 2 cups cubed and cooked chicken breast
- ¼ cup finely chopped celery
- ¼ cup fat-free mayonnaise
- ¾ tsp curry powder
- ¼ tsp fresh and finely grated lemon zest
- 8 slices freshly baked whole wheat bread
- 1/3 cup mango chutney
- 1 cup watercress
- 2 tbsp softened unsalted butter

**Instructions:**

Mix the chicken, celery, mayonnaise, lemon zest, and curry powder in a bowl.

Cook the mixture.

Spread 4 slices of bread with chutney.

Lay ½ cup of the salad and ¼ cup of the watercress.

Cover the ingredients with the remaining bread, then spread butter on the outer parts of the sandwich.

In a panini maker, cook the sandwich for 4 minutes.

Ensure the bread turns golden brown before removing it from the panini maker.

Serve and enjoy.

# 32. Turkey, Bacon and Feta Panini

What makes this recipe delicious is the combination of all bacon strips and the turkey. It is suitable for either breakfast or dinner. The crunchiness in this recipe results from the inclusion of the veggies.

**Servings:** 4

**Preparation time:** 20 minutes

**Ingredients:**

- 12 thick slices of applewood smoked bacon
- ¼ cup mayonnaise
- ¼ cup jellied cranberry sauce
- 8 slices sourdough bread
- Thinly sliced cooked turkey as you like
- 1 cup crumbled feta cheese
- 2 cups fresh baby spinach

**Instructions:**

Preheat your panini maker.

On a skillet, cook the bacon until it becomes crispy.

Remove the bacon, then place them on the paper towel to drain the dripping.

Mix the cranberry sauce and mayonnaise in a bowl to prepare a homemade sauce.

Apply the mayonnaise mixture on the bread slices.

Layer bacon, turkey, cheese, and spinach on four slices, then cover them with the remaining pieces of bread.

Transfer the sandwich to the panini maker, then cook for 5 minutes.

Ensure the cheese melts and the bread turns golden brown before serving.

# 33. Corned Beef Cheddar Panini

Do you need a quick snack because of your busy schedule? The Beef cheddar panini is the perfect recipe for you.

**Servings:** 4

**Preparation Time:** 17 minutes

**Ingredients:**

- 8 slices ciabatta
- Olive oil
- ¼ cup mayonnaise
- 8 slices provolone cheese
- 2 (14 oz) corned beef
- ¼ cup ketchup
- 1 peeled and thinly sliced medium white onion

**Ingredients:**

Preheat your panini maker.

Take the bread slices, then brush them with the oil.

Apply mayonnaise on 4 slices, then top with 2 cheese slices.

Divide the beef into the cheese slices, add ketchup, and finally the onion.

Cover the ingredients with the remaining slices of bread.

Cook the sandwich until it turns golden brown, and all the cheese gets to melt.

# 34. Margherita Panini

It is the ideal recipe that can set you up for great weekends. Prepare this for either dinner or breakfast on a Friday.

**Servings:** 4

**Preparation Time:** 15 minutes

**Ingredients:**

- 8 slices ciabatta
- 12 slices mozzarella cheese
- 4 thinly sliced red tomatoes
- Salt and freshly ground black pepper
- 8 basil leaves
- Olive oil

**Instructions:**

Preheat your panini maker.

On 4 slices of bread, place the cheese pieces.

Top with the tomatoes, then season with pepper and salt.

Distribute the basil leaves over the slices, then drizzle the oil over the ingredients.

Cover the ingredients with the other slices of bread.

Cook for about 5 minutes until the cheese melts and the bread turns golden brown.

# 35. Maple Blackberry Panini

Why don't you be adventurous and try making a panini with blackberries? These fruits' effect when you pair them with other ingredients is impressive.

**Servings:** 4

**Preparation Time:** 25 minutes

**Ingredients:**

- 8 slices ciabatta
- Olive oil
- 4 slices ham
- 2 pitted and thinly sliced peaches
- ½ cup halved blackberries
- 1 tbsp chopped basil
- 1/3 cup crumbled goat cheese
- ¼ cup grated cheddar cheese
- ¾ tsp maple syrup

**Instructions:**

Preheat your panini maker.

Take two slices of bread, then brush them with olive oil.

Lay a slice of ham on a single bread slice.

Top with some blackberries, peaches, goat cheese, basil, and cheddar cheese.

Drizzle the ingredients with olive oil and maple syrup.

Cover the ingredients with the other bread slice.

Cook it until it becomes golden brown.

Ensure the cheese melts and the berries get to burst some juice out.

Repeat the process with the remaining slices.

Serve and enjoy.

# 36. Bacon, Asparagus, and Mayo Panini

Do you have guests and have no idea of what to prepare for them to eat? These delicious Panini will make the visitors happy and yearning for more. They are great for lunch since they combine herbs and asparagus lining on the bacon and mayonnaise.

**Servings:** 4

**Preparation Time:** 20 minutes

**Ingredients:**

- 12 bacon slices
- ¼ lb. halved asparagus
- 2 tbsp olive oil
- A pinch of salt
- Freshly ground black pepper
- 8 ciabatta slices
- ½ cup garlic mayonnaise
- 1 tsp chopped parsley

**Instructions:**

Preheat your panini maker.

On a skillet, fry the bacon until they become crisp. Remove, then drain the bacon on a paper towel.

In a bowl, mix the asparagus, pepper, salt, and olive oil. Set the mixture aside.

Apply the mayonnaise on a slice of bread, then top it with 3 slices of bacon, line some asparagus in a layer. Apply more mayonnaise at the top, then sprinkle a little parsley on the ingredients.

Cover with the remaining bread slice.

Repeat the procedure with the remaining ingredients.

Cook the sandwich until they turn golden brown.

# 37. Zesty Crabmeat Panini

A fantastic combination of ingredients to come up with an excellent panini recipe. You should try this recipe out!

**Servings:** 4

**Preparation Time:** 15 minutes

**Ingredients:**

- 16 oz. lump crab meat
- Salt and freshly ground black pepper
- ¼ cup mayonnaise
- 1 zested and juiced lemon
- ¼ cup chopped green onion
- ¼ cup chopped parsley
- ½ tsp hot sauce
- 1 tsp Worcestershire sauce
- 8 slices ciabatta
- 2 tbsp melted butter

**Instructions:**

Preheat your panini press.

Combine the meat, mayonnaise, pepper, lemon zest, salt, lemon juice, hot sauce, green onion, Worcestershire sauce, and parsley in a bowl.

Take the bread slices, then brush both sides with butter.

Place the meat mixture on a single side of 4 bread slices, ensuring it is well spread.

Cover the ingredients with the remaining slices of bread.

Grill the sandwiches until they turn golden brown.

# 38. Roasted Vegetable Panini Bite

You should cook this recipe as it is the best panini appetizer when hosting parties. Decorate them with toothpicks at the center and serve with a mayonnaise dipping.

**Servings:** 2

**Preparation Time:** 10 minutes

**Ingredients:**

- 2 slices rustic Italian bread
- 4 ounces sliced mozzarella cheese
- Roasted tomatoes to taste
- Roasted asparagus to taste
- Roasted zucchini to taste
- Roasted mushrooms to taste
- Fresh basil leaves to taste
- 2 ounces prosciutto

**Instructions:**

Preheat your panini maker.

Place a slice on a flat surface, then top with cheese, asparagus, tomatoes, zucchini, prosciutto, basil, and mushroom.

You can add an extra cheese layer if you desire.

Cover the ingredients with the other slice of bread.

Cook for 4 minutes until the bread is golden brown.

Serve in bite-sized pieces.

# 39. Eggplant Panini

Eggplant adds creaminess to the sandwich making it more delicious. When serving, you can complement it with salad or fries.

**Servings:** 4

**Preparation Time:** 15 minutes

**Ingredients:**

- 1 small eggplant, cut into ¼" slices
- Salt and ground black pepper
- 2 oz. divided olive oil
- 1 loaf flatbread, cut into 4 horizontal slices
- 6 oz. sliced and drained jarred roasted red bell peppers
- 4 oz. shredded mozzarella cheese
- 2 oz. roasted garlic hummus

**Instructions:**

In a bowl, put the eggplant, then sprinkle it with pepper and salt. Set the eggplant aside for about 2 minutes to allow blending of the flavors.

On a frying pan with oil, sauté the eggplant for about 3 minutes on every side.

Preheat your panini press.

On a flat surface, place the bread, then layer aside with the red pepper, eggplant, and cheese.

Top the ingredients by spreading ½ oz. of the garlic on the other bread piece.

Cover the sandwich.

Grill it for about 6 minutes until the cheese gets to melt.

# 40. Sourdough Chipotle Chicken Panini

The amount of spice you would want to put in this recipe depends on whoever you are cooking for, but you can crank the amount up if you want.

**Servings:** 1

**Preparation Time:** 15 minutes

**Ingredients:**

- 2 slices sourdough bread
- 2 oz. Caesar salad dressing
- 1 cooked diced chicken breast
- 4 oz. shredded Cheddar cheese
- ½ oz. bacon bits
- ¼ oz. chipotle chili powder
- 1 oz. softened butter

**Instructions:**

Preheat your panini press.

On a flat surface, place the bread, then spread the salad dressing on every slice.

Top the dressing with cheese, chicken, bacon, and chipotle powder.

Use the other slices of bread to close the sandwich.

Apply butter on the outer surface of the bread.

Cook it in the panini press until the bread gets to toast.

# 41. Panzanella Panini

The ingredient in this recipe, Panzanella, originates from Italy. It is a significant summer dish that comprises tomatoes and stale bread. Try this recipe whenever you want to have the Italian feel.

**Servings:** 1

**Preparation Time:** 15 minutes

**Ingredients:**

- 1 French deli roll, halved
- 2 slices mozzarella cheese
- 4 fresh basil leaves
- 1 tsp balsamic vinegar
- 1 small sliced tomato
- ¼ tbsp olive oil

**Instructions:**

Preheat our Panini maker.

On a flat surface, place the roll facing upwards. Use balsamic vinegar to sprinkle to the cut sides of the roll.

Top the roll with a slice of cheese, tomato slices, basil, then cover with another slice of cheese.

Cover the ingredients with the other roll.

Cook for 4 minutes in the maker, ensuring the cheese melts and the roll turns golden brown.

## 42. Italian-Style Tuna Melt

The recipe is a classic type of tuna melt sandwich. It takes a short time to prepare and does not take a lot of mayonnaise.

**Servings:** 4

**Preparation Time:** 20 minutes

**Ingredients:**

- 2, 5 oz. cans drained tuna
- 1 diced small red onion
- ¼ cup chopped green olives
- 2 tbsp mayonnaise
- 2 tbsp bottled pesto
- 1 tbsp rinsed and chopped capers
- 1 fresh lemon juice
- 8 whole-wheat bread slices of bread
- 2 oz. low-fat mozzarella shreds
- 1 large sliced tomato
- 1 tsp olive oil

**Instructions:**

Mix the tuna, pesto, olives, mayonnaise, onions, capers, and lemon juice in a bowl. Stir the mixture.

On moderate heat, preheat a non-stick pan.

Coat it with oil.

Layer the tuna mixture on four bread slices, followed by tomato slices before topping with mozzarella shreds, then cover with the remaining slices.

Cook for 5 minutes on every side, ensuring the cheese gets to melt.

Serve and enjoy.

# 43. Cheddar – Turkey Panini

Want to try a crisp and tasty Panini recipe? Look no further as this recipe will suit all your needs. It is simple to prepare and takes a short time to cook.

**Servings:** 2

**Preparation Time: 20 minutes**

**Ingredients:**

- 4 slices brioche loaf
- 2 oz. cheddar cheese shreds
- 2 oz. thinly sliced smoked turkey
- 1 tbsp room-temperature unsalted butter
- 2 tbsp fruit preserves

**Instructions:**

Preheat your waffle iron.

Prepare 2 sandwiches by dividing the cheese and turkey between the slices.

Apply butter on the outer parts of the bread.

Cook for 5 minutes.

Serve the recipe alongside the fruit preserves.

# 44. Turkey & Swiss Reuben Sandwich

The recipe is an inspiration from a Jewish staple. It has very few calories, and half of the saturated fat in use is traditional.

**Servings:** 4

**Preparation Time:** 15 minutes

**Ingredients:**

- ¼ tsp Russian dressing
- ¼ tsp black pepper
- 1 lb. pastrami turkey
- 4 slices of low-fat Swiss cheese
- 8 toasted rye bread slices
- 1 cup bottled sauerkraut

**Instructions:**

On separate 4 plates, divide the pastrami.

Top the pastrami with cheese, then microwave them for 40 seconds per plate.

Lay the slices of bread on a flat surface.

Top the slices with some chunk of sauerkraut.

Add the cheese mixture, black, and use the dressing to top it.

Cover with the remaining bread slices.

Serve and enjoy.

# 45. Deli lamb Mayo Panini

Any Panini recipe with a lamb on the ingredient list is a delicious meal. It is super-fast to prepare this recipe, and the ingredients and readily available in a store near you.

**Servings:** 2

**Preparation Time:** 7 minutes

**Ingredients:**

- 2 pita ciabatta bread
- 4 slices deli lamb
- 4 tbsp arugula leaves
- 4 tbsp mayo
- 1 sliced red onion
- ½ tsp oregano
- ½ tsp rosemary
- Salt and black pepper

**Instructions:**

In a Panini maker, add the bread, then press for a minute.

Spread mayonnaise on the bread.

Add the arugula, lamb, onion, salt, rosemary, oregano, and pepper to the bread.

Cover the bread, then divide it into two.

Serve and enjoy.

# 46. Caramelized Onion Panini

The recipe is one of the various options for vegans. The recipe's primary ingredient is onion, which it transforms in a flavorful way.

**Servings:** 1

**Preparation Time:** 15 minutes

**Ingredients:**

- 2 ciabatta bread slices
- 2 sliced red onions
- 1 tbsp oil
- 1 tbsp butter
- 2 tbsp grated cheddar cheese
- ½ tsp garlic powder
- Salt and pepper
- ½ tsp thyme

**Instructions:**

Fry the onion in preheated pan with the oil until they get to caramelize.

Add garlic, thyme, pepper, and salt. Toss the mixture for 30 seconds.

Remove from the heat, then set aside.

Apply butter on the bread slices.

Add onion and cheese to the slices.

Cover the slices using the remaining one.

Cook in the Panini maker for a minute.

Serve and enjoy.

# 47. Sausage Spinach Panini

A perfect combination for a sandwich is ciabatta bread with sausage. The recipe also has parmesan cheese, spinach, and sesame seeds.

**Servings:** 1

**Preparation Time:** 10 minutes

**Ingredients:**

- 2 focaccia slices
- 2 roughly chopped sausages
- 2 tbsp spinach
- 2 tbsp grated parmesan cheese
- Salt and pepper
- 1 tsp butter

**Instructions:**

Melt the butter in a pan.

Cook the sausages in the pan for 2 minutes.

Add pepper and salt to the sausages, then toss for a minute.

Press the slices in a panini maker for a minute.

Add spinach, parmesan, and sausages on the slices, then cover with the remaining slice.

# 48. Spelt Spinach Mushroom Panini

Are you a healthy eater? If this category fits you, then this is the to-go recipe. The recipe has a combination of mushroom, ciabatta bread, cheddar cheese, and spinach.

**Servings:** 2

**Preparation Time:** 15 minutes

**Ingredients:**

- 2 spelt ciabatta bread slices
- ½ cup sliced mushroom
- 1 chopped onion
- ½ cup chopped spinach
- 2 cheddar cheese slices
- 1 tsp chili flakes
- 1 tsp olive oil
- Salt and black pepper

**Instructions:**

Preheat the oil in a pan.

Cook the onion in the pan until it gets to caramelize.

Add mushroom to the pan, then stir as it cooks for 3 minutes.

Add spinach, pepper, chili flakes, and salt.

Toss the mixture for 3 minutes.

Remove from the heat, then add the mix to the bread slice.

Top it with the cheese, then cover with the remaining bread slice.

Cook it in the panini maker for 2 minutes.

# 49. Fig and Artichoke Panini

Another great combination for a panini is the inclusion of fig and artichoke. The addition of cheese and other spices enriches the flavor of the sandwich.

**Servings:** 2

**Preparation Time:** 20 minutes

**Ingredients:**

- 2 ciabatta bread slices
- ½ cup diced artichoke hearts
- ½ cup sliced fig
- 1 tsp soy sauce
- 1 tsp chopped parsley
- 1 tsp paprika
- 4 tbsp grated mozzarella cheese
- Salt and pepper
- 1 tbsp butter

**Instructions:**

In a pan, melt the butter.

Cook the artichoke in the pan for 2 minutes.

Add in the fig, then stir to mix for another 2 minutes.

Add salt, soy sauce, pepper, parsley, and paprika.

Cook for another 2 minutes.

Spread the artichoke mixture onto a single bread slice.

Top with the cheese, then cover with the other bread slice.

Cook it in the panini maker for 2 minutes.

# 50. Chocolate Panini

Chocolate as a main ingredient never fails a recipe. It is a treat that one can prepare for dinner or breakfast. Cooking this for your family and will leave them yearning for more.

**Servings:** 2

**Preparation Time:** 15 minutes

**Ingredients:**

- 2 tsp softened unsalted butter
- 2 pieces great white slices of bread
- ½ tsp fine-tuned sugar
- 1 tbsp low-fat lotion cheese softened
- 4 oz. semi-sweet chocolate
- ½ cup fresh-picked and cut strawberries
- ¼ cup strongly whipped heavy whipping cream

**Instructions:**

Apply butter on every side of the bread slices, then sprinkle the sugar on the bread.

Spread the cheese on every side of the slices.

Place the chocolate bar on the side of the bread slice with cheese, then cover with the remaining slice.

Cook in a panini maker for 3 minutes, ensuring the bread turns golden brown and the bar gets to melt.

Divide the sandwich into two, then top it with whipped cream and strawberries.

# 51. Southwestern Panini

When you are very busy, this recipe comes in handy for you as it takes a short time to prepare. In addition, it looks not only appealing but also has excellent taste.

**Servings:** 4

**Preparation Time:** 20 minutes

**Ingredients:**

- 1 freshly peeled ripe avocado
- ½ tsp refined sugar
- ½ tsp garlic salt
- ½ tsp freshly grated lemon juice
- 8 slices freshly baked oat bread
- 250g thinly sliced deli ham
- 4 slices Swiss cheese
- 1 tbsp unsalted butter

**Instructions:**

Put the avocado, sugar, salt, and lemon juice in a bowl.

Mash the mixture until it forms a pleasing combination.

Spread the avocado mixture on 4 slices.

Top with the cheese and ham, then cover with the remaining slices.

Apply butter on both sides of the sandwich.

Cook on a grill for 3 minutes.

# 52. Chicken Florentine Panini

The recipe originates from an ancient recipe from Italy. What makes it unique is the mixture of cheese, chicken, onion, and spinach. You can serve this recipe with some extra sauce to enhance the flavor.

**Servings:** 4

**Preparation Time:** 25 minutes

**Ingredients:**

- 1 (5 oz.) can baby spinach fresh
- ¼ cup softened butter
- 8 slices sourdough bread
- ¼ cup salad dressing, creamy
- 8 slices Italian Provolone cheese
- 250g shaved deli chicken
- 2 pieces sliced red onion

**Instructions:**

In a skillet, sauté the spinach in oil until it gets to wilt.

After 2 minutes, drain, then wipe clean the skillet.

On 4 slices of bread, top the slices with the salad dressing, then a slice of cheese.

Top with spinach, onion, deli chicken, and an extra cheese slice.

Cover the ingredients with the rest of the bread slices, then apply butter on the outer part of the sandwich.

Cook in a panini maker for 5 minutes.

# 53. Apple Pie Panini a La Mode

The recipe will leave you thinking of your childhood memories. It is a delicious snack for either breakfast or dessert.

**Servings:** 2

**Preparation Time:** 15 Minutes

**Ingredients:**

- ¼ cup softened mascarpone cheese
- 1 tsp runny honey
- 2 tbsp softened salted butter
- 4 thick slices cinnamon bread
- ½ thinly sliced green apple
- 1 tbsp light brown sugar
- 2 large scoops of vanilla ice cream

**Instructions:**

Preheat your panini maker.

Add the honey and cheese to a food processor, then process the mixture until it becomes fluffy and well mixed.

On every bread slice, apply butter.

Flip the bread slices, then apply the mascarpone, making the inner sides.

Top two slices with apple, then cover with the remaining slices.

On the sandwich, sprinkle the sugar on all sides.

Cook the sandwich for 4 minutes.

Serve the sandwiches on different plates, then top with a generous vanilla ice cream.

## 54. Banana Brûlée Croissant Panini

The recipe is fancy as it consists of rich ingredients. However, the preparation is easy and takes a short time to cook.

**Servings:** 1

**Preparation Time:** 15 minutes

**Ingredients:**

- 3 tbsp salted almond butter
- 1 cooled and halved freshly baked croissant
- 1 peeled and sliced medium ripe banana
- 1 tbsp light brown sugar

**Instructions:**

Preheat our Panini maker.

Apply the butter on both slices evenly.

On a single slice, arrange the slices of banana.

Top with a sugar sprinkle, then burn them with a kitchen torch to melt the sugar.

Cover the ingredients with the remaining croissant slice.

Cook for 4 minutes.

Serve and enjoy.

# 55. Mallow, Hazelnut, and Banana

A combination of the listed ingredients makes this delicious Panini recipe perfect for breakfast and dinner snacks.

**Servings:** 2

**Preparation Time:** 15mins

**Ingredients:**

- 1 cup hazelnut spread
- 8 slices white bread, cut ½ inch thick
- 2 peeled and sliced bananas
- 16 halved marshmallows
- Softened butter
- Powdered sugar

**Instructions:**

Preheat our panini maker.

In a bowl, warm the hazelnut, then spread it on every bread slice.

Top 4 slices with banana, then cover the remaining slices with marshmallows.

Bring the two sets of slices together to form a sandwich.

Apply the butter on both sides of the sandwich using a brush.

Cook the sandwich for 5 minutes.

Remove from the maker, then sprinkle the sugar on the sandwich.

Serve and enjoy.

# 56. PB&J Panini

The recipe has an upgrade from the standard types. The peanut butter, cinnamon bread, and raspberry jelly add a unique taste and flavor.

**Servings:** 1

**Preparation Time:** 12mins

**Ingredients:**

- 2 tbsp smooth peanut butter
- 2 slices cinnamon bread
- 1 tbsp raspberry jelly

**Instructions:**

Preheat our panini maker.

Apply the peanut to a slice of the bread.

On the other slice, apply the raspberry.

Bring the slices together to make a sandwich.

Cook for 4 minutes, then let the sandwich cool for 2 minutes.

Divide it into half.

Serve and enjoy.

# 57. Grilled Chicken Panini

It is a unique delicacy that is suitable for the whole family. It takes a short time to prepare and cook, making it ideal for busy schedules.

**Servings:** 1

**Preparation Time:** 10 Minutes

**Ingredients:**

- 2 thick slices of bread
- 2 tbsp basil butter
- 1 piece boneless and skinless grilled chicken breast
- 1 pickle halved
- 1 slice Swiss cheese
- ½ tsp chili powder
- Dash black pepper

**Basil Butter**

- 1 stick butter
- 4 finely diced medium-large basil leaves

**Instructions:**

For the basil butter, melt the butter in a pan.

Add the basil.

Stir the mixture, then transfer it to a bowl.

Transfer it to a refrigerator and leave it until it becomes hardened.

On the bread slices, apply the butter, then top with half of the chicken.

Add the cheese, pickle, chili powder, and black pepper to the slices.

Cook the sandwich in a panini maker for 5 minutes.

# 58. Kicking Bacon Panini

Do you love spicy foods? If that's your portion, this is the recipe to suit your desires.

**Servings:** 1

**Preparation Time:** 15 Minutes

**Ingredients:**

- 2 thick slices of bread
- 1 tbsp divided sriracha sauce
- 4 slices turkey bacon
- 2 slices onion
- 2 diced jalapenos
- 2/3 tsp cayenne powder
- 1 slice queso cheese

**Instructions:**

On a flat surface lay the bread slices.

Apply the sriracha on both slices.

Top it with half of the bacon, jalapenos, onion, cheese, and cayenne powder.

Bring the slices together to make a sandwich.

Cook on a grill for 4 minutes on every side.

# 59. Cordon Bleu Panini

The Cordon Blue panini is a noon-time snack for the family as it is delicious and simple to prepare.

**Servings:** 1

**Preparation Time:** 15 Minutes

**Ingredients:**

- 2 slices thick bread
- 1 oz. pre-cooked diced chicken
- 1 oz. pre-cooked diced ham
- 1 oz. diced celery
- ½ can (6 oz.) condensed cream chicken soup
- 1 oz. shredded parmesan

**Instructions:**

Mix the ham, chicken, chicken soup, and celery in a bowl.

Spread the chicken mixture on a slice of bread, then top with cheese.

Bring the slices together, then cook the sandwich in a panini maker for 5 minutes.

Serve and enjoy.

# Conclusion

If you love Paninis, then you need to have a great recipe collection at your disposal. This book will give you everything you need to make great-tasting sandwiches for breakfast, lunch, or dinner. You will find a variety of recipes that taste wonderful. Whether you like hot meat filling with melted cheese or fish that has been seasoned with your favorite herbs, it's all in this book. Each recipe will treat your palate and give you something to smile about.

Thank you again for downloading this book. I hope you enjoy it!

# About the Author

Angel Burns learned to cook when she worked in the local seafood restaurant near her home in Hyannis Port in Massachusetts as a teenager. The head chef took Angel under his wing and taught the young woman the tricks of the trade for cooking seafood. The skills she had learned at a young age helped her get accepted into Boston University's Culinary Program where she also minored in business administration.

Summers off from school meant working at the same restaurant but when Angel's mentor and friend retired as head chef, she took over after graduation and created classic and new dishes that delighted the diners. The restaurant flourished under Angel's culinary creativity and one customer developed more than an appreciation for Angel's food. Several months after taking over the position, the young woman met her future husband at work and they have been inseparable ever since. They still live in Hyannis Port with their two children and a cocker spaniel named Buddy.

Angel Burns turned her passion for cooking and her business acumen into a thriving e-book business. She has authored several successful books on cooking different types of dishes using simple ingredients for novices and experienced chefs alike. She is still head chef in Hyannis Port and says she will probably never leave!

# Author's Afterthoughts

With so many books out there to choose from, I want to thank you for choosing this one and taking precious time out of your life to buy and read my work. Readers like you are the reason I take such passion in creating these books.

It is with gratitude and humility that I express how honored I am to become a part of your life and I hope that you take the same pleasure in reading this book as I did in writing it.

Can I ask one small favour? I ask that you write an honest and open review on Amazon of what you thought of the book. This will help other readers make an informed choice on whether to buy this book.

*My sincerest thanks,*

*Angel Burns*

If you want to be the first to know about news, new books, events and giveaways, subscribe to my newsletter by clicking the link below

*https://angel-burns.gr8.com*

**or Scan QR-code**

Printed in Poland
by Amazon Fulfillment
Poland Sp. z o.o., Wrocław
22 June 2024